Penguin Modern Poets

— **9** —

DENISE LEVERTOV
KENNETH REXROTH
WILLIAM CARLOS WILLIAMS

D1419778

Penguin Books

Penguin Books Ltd, Harmondsworth, Middlesex, England
Penguin Books Australia Ltd, Ringwood, Victoria, Australia

—

This selection first published 1967
Reprinted 1968

—

Copyright © Penguin Books, 1967

—

Made and printed in Great Britain
by Cox & Wyman Ltd, London, Fakenham and Reading
Set in Monotype Garamond

Contents

ACKNOWLEDGEMENTS

For permission to reprint copyright material the following acknowledgements are made: for poems by Denise Levertov to Jonathan Cape (*The Jacob's Ladder*) and New Directions (*O Taste and See* and *With Eyes at the Back of Our Heads*); for poems by Kenneth Rexroth to New Directions (*The Art of Worldly Wisdom, Complete Shorter Poems, In What Hour, One Hundred Poems from the Japanese, The Phoenix and the Tortoise,* and *The Signature of All Things*); for poems by William Carlos Williams to MacGibbon & Kee (*Collected Earlier Poems, Collected Later Poems, Paterson,* and *Pictures from Breughel*).

DENISE LEVERTOV

Lonely Man

An open world
    within its mountain rim:
trees on the plain lifting
    their heads, fine strokes
    of grass stretching themselves to breathe
the last of the light.
                Where a man
riding horseback raises dust
    under the eucalyptus trees, a long way off, the dust
is gray-gold, a cloud
    of pollen. A field
    of cosmea turns
    all its many faces
of wide-open flowers west, to the light.

It is your loneliness
your energy
      baffled in the stillness
    gives an edge to the shadows –
the great sweep of mountain shadow,
shadows of ants and leaves,
    the stones of the road each with its shadow
and you with your long shadow
closing your book and standing up
to stretch, your long shadow-arms
    stretching back of you, baffled.

The Sage

The cat is eating the roses:
that's the way he is.
Don't stop him, don't stop
the world going round,
that's the way things are.
The third of May
was misty; fourth of May
who knows. Sweep
the rose-meat up, throw the bits
out in the rain.
He never eats
every crumb, says
the hearts are bitter.
That's the way he is, he knows
the world and the weather.

The Communion

A pondering frog looks
out from my eyes:

dark-red, veiled blue, plums
roll to the center of a bowl

and at close horizon water-towers
hump and perch.

           Leap
frog, to a lake: leaves
support the lilies, water holds

erect the long, strong stems,
reflects gleaming

rosy petals, pollen-yellow lily-buds,
clouds lilac-tinted and dissolving.
Back to the plums –

eggs in a blue nest – the squat
peaked assembly of towers.

What is it?
           An accord.

Break out, frog,
sing, you who don't know

anything about anything.
'To dance without moving' shall be your burden.

Bread

As florid berries to the oak, should I pin
sequins to this Rockland County bouquet
of bare twigs? – as roses
to pineboughs? – While a primrose-yellow
apple, flushed with success, levitates quietly
in the top right-hand corner of a small canvas,
giving pleasure by its happiness?
But these are thin pleasures, to content
the contented. For hunger:
the bare stretching thorny branches that may never speak
though they conceal or half-reveal
sharp small syllables of bud; and the ragged laughter
– showing gaps between its teeth –
of the anonymous weeds, towsle-heads,
yellow-brown like the draggled undersides of
dromedary and llama basking
proud and complete in airy wedges
of April sun – something
of endurance, to endure
ripeness if it come, or suffer
a slow spring with lifted head –
a good crust of brown bread for the hungry.

To the Snake

Green Snake, when I hung you round my neck
and stroked your cold, pulsing throat
      as you hissed to me, glinting
arrowy gold scales, and I felt
      the weight of you on my shoulders,
and the whispering silver of your dryness
      sounded close at my ears –

Green Snake – I swore to my companions that certainly
      you were harmless! But truly
I had no certainty, and no hope, only desiring
      to hold you, for that joy,
               which left
a long wake of pleasure, as the leaves moved
and you faded into the pattern
of grass and shadows, and I returned
smiling and haunted, to a dark morning.

The Goddess

She in whose lipservice
I passed my time,
whose name I knew, but not her face,
came upon me where I lay in Lie Castle!

Flung me across the room, and
room after room (hitting the walls, re-
bounding – to the last
sticky wall – wrenching away from it
pulled hair out!)
till I lay
outside the outer walls!

There in cold air
lying still where her hand had thrown me,
I tasted the mud that splattered my lips:
the seeds of a forest were in it,
asleep and growing! I tasted
her power!

The silence was answering my silence,
a forest was pushing itself
out of sleep between my submerged fingers.

I bit on a seed and it spoke on my tongue
of day that shone already among stars
in the water-mirror of low ground,
and a wind rising ruffled the lights:
she passed near me returning from the encounter,
she who plucked me from the close rooms,

without whom nothing
flowers, fruits, sleeps in season,
without whom nothing
speaks in its own tongue, but returns
lie for lie!

Under the Tree

Under an orange-tree –
not one especial singular
orange-tree, but one among

the dark multitude. Recline
there, with a stone winejar

and the sense
of another dream
concentration would capture –
but it doesn't matter –

and the sense
of dust on the grass, of infinitesimal
flowers, of
cracks in the earth

and urgent life
passing there, ants and transparent
winged beings in their intensity
traveling from blade to blade,

under a modest orange-tree
neither lower nor taller
neither darker-leaved nor aglow
more beneficently

than the dark multitude
glowing in numberless lanes
the orange-farmer counts, but
not you – recline

and drink wine – the stone
will keep it cold – with the sense
of life yet to be lived – rest, rest,
the grass is growing –

let the oranges
ripen, ripen above you,
you are living too, one
among the dark multitude –

A Common Ground

I

To stand on common ground
here and there gritty with pebbles
yet elsewhere 'fine and mellow –
uncommon fine for ploughing'

there to labor
planting the vegetable words
diversely in their order
that they come to virtue!

To reach those shining pebbles,
that soil where uncommon men
have labored in their virtue
and left a store

of seeds for planting!
To crunch on words
grown in grit or fine
crumbling earth, sweet

to eat and sweet
to be given, to be eaten
in common, by laborer
and hungry wanderer . . .

2

In time of blossoming,
of red
buds, of red
margins upon
white petals among the
new green, of coppery
leaf-buds still weakly
folded, fuzzed
with silver hairs –

when on the grass verges
or elephant-hide rocks, the lunch hour
expands, the girls
laugh at the sun, men
in business suits awkwardly
recline, the petals
float and fall into
crumpled wax-paper, cartons
of hot coffee –

to speak as the sun's
deep tone of May gold speaks
or the spring chill in the rock's shadow,
a piercing minor scale running across the flesh
aslant – or petals
that dream their way
(speaking by being white
by being
curved, green-centered, falling
already while their tree
is half-red with buds) into

human lives! Poems stirred
into paper coffee-cups, eaten
with petals on rye in the
sun – the cold shadows in back,
and the traffic grinding the
borders of spring – entering
human lives forever,
unobserved, a spring element . . .

3

> . . . everything in the world must
> excel itself to be itself.
>
> *Pasternak*

Not 'common speech'
a dead level
but the uncommon speech of paradise,
tongue in which oracles
speak to beggars and pilgrims:

not illusion but what Whitman called
'the path
between reality and the soul',
a language
excelling itself to be itself,

speech akin to the light
with which at day's end and day's
renewal, mountains
sing to each other across the cold valleys.

The Rainwalkers

An old man whose black face
shines golden-brown as wet pebbles
under the streetlamp, is walking
two mongrel dogs of dis-
proportionate size, in the rain,
in the relaxed early-evening avenue.

The small sleek one wants to stop,
docile to the imploring soul of the trashbasket,
but the young tall curly one
wants to walk on; the glistening sidewalk
entices him to arcane happenings.

Increasing rain. The old bareheaded man
smiles and grumbles to himself.
The lights change: the avenue's
endless nave echoes notes of
liturgical red. He drifts

between his dogs' desires.
The three of them are enveloped –
turning now to go crosstown – in their
sense of each other, of pleasure,
of weather, of corners,
of leisurely tensions between them
and private silence.

In Memory of Boris Pasternak

I

The day before he died, a burnet moth
come to town perhaps on a load of greens,
took me a half-hour out of my way, or what
I'd thought was my way. It lay bemused
on the third step down of the subway entrance.
I took it up – it scarcely fluttered. Where
should I take it for safety,
away from hasty feet and rough hands?
We went through the hot streets together,
it lay trustingly in my hand,
awkwardly I shielded it from the dusty
wind, a glitter of brine
hovered about the cement vistas.
At last I found
a scrap of green garden
to hide the stranger, and silently took leave.

Not his soul –
I knew that dwelled always on Russian earth
– yet it was spoken in me
that the dark, narrow-winged, richly
crimson-signed being, an
apparition at the steps to the underworld,
whose need took me upwards again and further than
I had thought to walk, was a word,
an emanation from him, fulfilling
what he had written – 'I feel
that we shall be friends.'

2

Seen through what seem
his eyes (his gift) the gray barn
and the road into the forest,
the snipe's dead young I am burying among
wild-strawberry leaves, all
lifts itself, poises itself to speak:

and the deaf soul
struggles, strains forward, to lip-read what it needs:
and something is said, quickly,
in words of cloud-shadows moving and
the unmoving turn of the road, something
not quite caught, but filtered
through some outpost of dreaming sense
the gist, the drift. I remember
a dream two nights ago: the voice,
'the artist must
create himself or be born again'.

The Necessity

From love one takes
petal to rock and blesséd
away towards
descend,

one took thought
for frail tint and spectral
glisten, trusted
from way back that stillness,

one knew
that heart of fire, rose
at the core of gold glow,
could go down undiminished,

for love and
or if in fear knowing
the risk, knowing
what one is touching, one does it,

each part
of speech a spark
awaiting redemption, each
a virtue, a power

in abeyance unless we
give it care
our need designs in us. Then
all we have led away returns to us.

Matins

I

The authentic! Shadows of it
sweep past in dreams, one could say imprecisely,
evoking the almost-silent
ripping apart of giant
sheets of cellophane. No.
It thrusts up close. Exactly in dreams
it has you off-guard, you
recognize it before you have time.
For a second before waking
the alarm bell is a red conical hat, it
takes form.

2

The authentic! I said
rising from the toilet seat.
The radiator in rhythmic knockings
spoke of the rising steam.
The authentic, I said
breaking the handle of my hairbrush as I
brushed my hair in
rhythmic strokes: That's it,
that's joy, it's always
a recognition, the known
appearing fully itself, and
more itself than one knew.

3

The new day rises
as heat rises,

knocking in the pipes
with rhythms it seizes for its own
to speak of its invention –
the real, the new-laid
egg whose speckled shell
the poet fondles and must break
if he will be nourished.

4

A shadow painted where
yes, a shadow must fall.
The cow's breath
not forgotten in the mist, in the
words. Yes,
verisimilitude draws up
heat in us, zest
to follow through,
follow through,
follow
transformations of day
in its turning, in its becoming.

5

Stir the holy grains, set
the bowls on the table and
call the child to eat.

While we eat we think,
as we think an undercurrent
of dream runs through us
faster than thought
towards recognition.

Call the child to eat,
send him off, his mouth
tasting of toothpaste, to go down
into the ground, into a roaring train
and to school.

His cheeks are pink
his black eyes hold his dreams, he has left
forgetting his glasses.

Follow down the stairs at a clatter
to give them to him and save
his clear sight.

Cold air
comes in at the street door.

6

The authentic! It rolls
just out of reach, beyond
running feet and
stretching fingers, down
the green slope and into
the black waves of the sea.
Speak to me, little horse, beloved,
tell me
how to follow the iron ball,
how to follow through to the country
beneath the waves
to the place where I must kill you and you step out
of your bones and flystrewn meat
tall, smiling, renewed,
formed in your own likeness.

7

Marvelous Truth, confront us
at every turn,
in every guise, iron ball,
egg, dark horse, shadow,
cloud
of breath on the air,

dwell
in our crowded hearts
our steaming bathrooms, kitchens full of
things to be done, the
ordinary streets.

Thrust close your smile
that we know you, terrible joy.

A Solitude

A blind man. I can stare at him
ashamed, shameless. Or does he know it?
No, he is in a great solitude.

O, strange joy,
to gaze my fill at a stranger's face.
No, my thirst is greater than before.

In his world he is speaking
almost aloud. His lips move.
Anxiety plays about them. And now joy

of some sort trembles into a smile.
A breeze I can't feel
crosses that face as if it crossed water.

The train moves uptown, pulls in and
pulls out of the local stops. Within its loud
jarring movement a quiet,

the quiet of people not speaking,
some of them eyeing the blind man,
only a moment though, not thirsty like me,

and within that quiet his
different quiet, not quiet at all, a tumult
of images, but what are his images,

he is blind? He doesn't care
that he looks strange, showing
his thoughts on his face like designs of light

flickering on water, for he doesn't know
what look is.
I see he has never seen.

And now he rises, he stands at the door ready,
knowing his station is next. Was he counting?
No, that was not his need.

When he gets out I get out.
'Can I help you towards the exit?'
'Oh, alright.' An indifference.

But instantly, even as he speaks,
even as I hear indifference, his hand
goes out, waiting for me to take it,

and now we hold hands like children.
His hand is warm and not sweaty,
the grip firm, it feels good.

And when we have passed through the turnstile,
he going first, his hand at once
waits for mine again.

'Here are the steps. And here we turn
to the right. More stairs now.' We go
up into sunlight. He feels that,

the soft air. 'A nice day,
isn't it?' says the blind man. Solitude
walks with me, walks

beside me, he is not with me, he continues
his thoughts alone. But his hand and mine
know one another,

it's as if my hand were gone forth
on its own journey. I see him
across the street, the blind man,

and now he says he can find his way. He knows
where he is going, it is nowhere, it is filled
with presences. He says, *I am*.

Song for Ishtar

The moon is a sow
and grunts in my throat
Her great shining shines through me
so the mud of my hollow gleams
and breaks in silver bubbles

She is a sow
and I a pig and a poet

When she opens her white
lips to devour me I bite back
and laughter rocks the moon

In the black of desire
we rock and grunt, grunt and
shine

The Ache of Marriage

The ache of marriage:

thigh and tongue, beloved,
are heavy with it,
it throbs in the teeth

We look for communion
and are turned away, beloved,
each and each

It is leviathan and we
in its belly
looking for joy, some joy
not to be known outside it

two by two in the ark of
the ache of it.

A Figure of Time

Old Day the gardener seemed
Death himself, or Time, scythe in hand

by the sundial and freshly-dug
grave in my book of parables.

The mignonette, the dusty miller and silvery
rocks in the garden next door

thrived in his care (the rocks
not hidden by weeds but clear-

cut between tufts
of fern and saxifrage). Now

by our peartree with pruning-hook,
now digging the Burnes's neat, weedless

rosebeds, or as he peered
at a bird in Mrs Peach's laburnum,

his tall stooped person appeared, and gray
curls. He worked

slow and in silence, and knew perhaps
every garden around the block, gardens

we never saw, each one,
bounded by walls of old brick,

a square plot that was
world to itself.

When I was grown
and gone from home he remembered me

in the time of my growing, and sent,
year by year, salutations,

until there was no one there, in
changed times, to send them by. Old Day,

old Death, dusty
gardener, are you

alive yet, do I live on
yet, in your gray

considering eye?

The Novel

A wind is blowing. The book being written
shifts, halts, pages
yellow and white drawing apart
and inching together in
new tries. A single white half sheet
skims out under the door.

And cramped in their not yet
halfwritten lives, a man and a woman
grimace in pain. Their cat
yawning its animal secret,
stirs in the monstrous limbo of erasure.
They live (when they live) in fear

of blinding, of burning, of choking under a
mushroom cloud in the year of the roach.
And they want (like us) the eternity
of today, they want this fear to be
struck out at once by a thick black
magic marker, everywhere, every page,

the whole sheets of it crushed, crackling,
and tossed in the fire
        and when they were fine ashes
        the stove would cool and be cleaned
        and a jar of flowers would be put to stand
        on top of the stove in the spring light.

Meanwhile from page to page they
buy things, acquiring the look of a
full life; they argue, make silence bitter,
plan journeys, move house, implant

despair in each other
and then in the nick of time

they save one another with tears,
remorse, tenderness –
hooked on those wonder-drugs.
Yet they do have –
don't they – like us –
their days of grace, they

halt, stretch, a vision
breaks in on the cramped grimace,
inscape of transformation.
Something sundered begins to knit.
By scene, by sentence, something is rendered
back into life, back to the gods.

Hypocrite Women

Hypocrite women, how seldom we speak
of our own doubts, while dubiously
we mother man in his doubt!

And if at Mill Valley perched in the trees
the sweet rain drifting through western air
a white sweating bull of a poet told us

our cunts are ugly – why didn't we
admit we have thought so too? (And
what shame? They are not for the eye!)

No, they are dark and wrinkled and hairy,
caves of the Moon . . .   And when a
dark humming fills us, a

coldness towards life,
we are too much women to
own to such unwomanliness.

Whorishly with the psychopomp
we play and plead – and say
nothing of this later.   And our dreams,

with what frivolity we have pared them
like toenails, clipped them like ends of
split hair.

Our Bodies

Our bodies, still young under
the engraved anxiety of our
faces, and innocently

more expressive than faces:
nipples, navel, and pubic hair
make anyway a

sort of face: or taking
the rounded shadows at
breast, buttock, balls,

the plump of my belly, the
hollow of your
groin, as a constellation,

how it leans from earth to
dawn in a gesture of
play and

wise compassion –
nothing like this
comes to pass
in eyes or wistful
mouths.
    I have

a line or groove I love
runs down
my body from breastbone
to waist. It speaks of
eagerness, of
distance.

Your long back,
the sand color and
how the bones show, say

what sky after sunset
almost white
over a deep woods to which

rooks are homing, says.

KENNETH REXROTH

In the Memory of Andrée Rexroth

a

is a question of mutual being
a question of congruence or
proximity a question of
a sudden passage in air beyond
a window a long controlled fall
of music or is congruence
an infusion illumination have
you waited at places have
you seen places have
you said where have
you said adverbs now
air goes up and in glitter
out of mossy darkness memory
more real than anything
anything that ever was in all
the world and they shall
find at least these bodies broken against
no fact and no dream

b   a lamb in the distance

On the reality of loss and tense
and the participation of loss and tense
where loss is an imagined real
and tense may break in case
i.e.: as aorist breaks in instrumentals
dative garment and ablative
informant. Distinguish that the problem is not
of being and the dilemma is
not scalar and it is not differences

but distinctions that matter, for
there can be no avoirdupois
of location, nor metric of purpose except
as contingent to mensurand. As
death, an objective
and spasm.

Thus a present; the water-buckle and night
as a fist or from the local an express
        face pulls
away in the subway. There are
conversely, no rulers in instants,
for susceptibility to temporal position
is either habit or donation
and reveals primes,
gratuity and volition

c   a time

take one
from a pair a pair
from a quartette a quartette
from an
octette
the arrow through the octave
and the sun rising athwart
the ungloved thighs
the diamond refracted in honey
creep in thought
the minute spider creeps on the
eyeball the glass
rod swinging descends
ultimately to be
refracted in the pale

luminous solution
hair pulled by the wind
eyeballs flaked with light
the two princesses fall
from the ether of intensity
to the ether of irrevocables
and the yellow
animal climbs the cascade in the secret
interior of the highest
mountain.

d

cause of a difficulty
trauma of the word
conflicts the eyes the clocks makes
morning pale makes artifacts
of cause so one a deep
so a single fact cool
one a person it was
then a time then and
a position not the same position
as formerly not the unknown
causes of slight cool being
not the cleave the borders
one pull the somatic anemone
or a person she interprets
this objectification as the interest
of a body being a place being
one a person a woman undertakes
this a thing an understood touched
artifact being more substantial
as having evolved out of
process and generally

not anticipated when
arrived not fully
understood

e

for an abrupt
conscious adjustment externalizes
shoulders instants and graces not
of a joy of being in one place and
then in another but of being
profoundly in one place thinking a
place internally
return to an irrevocable body
to the perpetuity of a death
to a gong in a dream
as there is a qualitative difference
between two stars, and a tightening
incline as result of thought
brilliant infinitesimals so now
undulant and cold this is displayed
as a field for a unique progress as a
quality of atmosphere measurable
and inescapable nothing can
foreclose this crism nothing
can withstand for long memory
always awakens this usufruct
is held by a very old very endurable
meaning

Autumn in California

Autumn in California is a mild
And anonymous season, hills and valleys
Are colorless then, only the sooty green
Eucalyptus, the conifers and oaks sink deep
Into the haze; the fields are plowed, bare, waiting;
The steep pastures are tracked deep by the cattle;
There are no flowers, the herbage is brittle.
All night along the coast and the mountain crests
Birds go by, murmurous, high in the warm air.
Only in the mountain meadows the aspens
Glitter like goldfish moving up swift water;
Only in the desert villages the leaves
Of the cottonwoods descend in smoky air.

  Once more I wander in the warm evening
Calling the heart to order and the stiff brain
To passion. I should be thinking of dreaming, loving,
    dying,
Beauty wasting through time like draining blood,
And me alone in all the world with pictures
Of pretty women and the constellations.
But I hear the clocks in Barcelona strike at dawn
And the whistles blowing for noon in Nanking.
I hear the drone, the snapping high in the air
Of planes fighting, the deep reverberant
Grunts of bombardment, the hasty clamor
Of anti-aircraft.

                        In Nanking at the first bomb,
A moon-faced, willowy young girl runs into the street,
Leaves her rice bowl spilled and her children crying,
And stands stiff, cursing quietly, her face raised to the sky.
Suddenly she bursts like a bag of water,
And then as the blossom of smoke and dust diffuses,

The walls topple slowly over her.
                                    I hear the voices
Young, fatigued and excited, of two comrades
In a closed room in Madrid. They have been up
All night, talking of trout in the Pyrenees,
Spinoza, old nights full of riot and sherry,
Women they might have had or almost had,
Picasso, Velasquez, relativity.
The candlelight reddens, blue bars appear
In the cracks of the shutters, the bombardment
Begins again as though it had never stopped,
The morning wind is cold and dusty,
Their furloughs are over. They are shock troopers,
They may not meet again. The dead light holds
In impersonal focus the patched uniforms,
The dog-eared copy of Lenin's Imperialism,
The heavy cartridge belt, holster and black revolver butt.
    The moon rises late over Mt Diablo,
Huge, gibbous, warm; the wind goes out,
Brown fog spreads over the bay from the marshes,
And overhead the cry of birds is suddenly
Loud, wiry, and tremulous.

Dative Haruspices

Film and filament, no
Donor, gift without
Reciprocity, transparent
Tactile act, an imaginary
Web of structure sweeps
The periphery of being, glass
Entities point, the fundamental
Entails arise, ominous
Real, augurs move in sleep
Voices break the vast
Indifferent sarcophagus, this
Source and word, secret, never
Fractured by volition
Seventy years
Hidden, the hangman
In the navel, or
An eye in the oblivion
Of an instantaneous
Being of a differential
Flexible beyond assent
Sentient webs morseled with fact
Parcel now in the sky, compact
Parabolas branch in a capsule
Punctured with instants, ominous of items
Stars Palps Needles
Where the central summation extrudes
Inhibited muscular tensors, what
Recall of pentacles, bulbs
Uttered in scissors loan, are being
Is sown on the rent
Tumuli, what ing in the ever
Lasting (there are no horizons

In mountains, but
Dispersed minutes itemize the skyline, stones
Are accepted by canyons with uniform
Acceleration and snow
Disturbed by wind hovers in sun
Light in the passes) directrices
Of becoming, courteous
In the differentials
With what fact
For an endless time being
Watching luminous songs utter
The round earth visible
As the moon moves
Men move from a distance
Men sleep overhead
A word a fire
Occurs endures for
Generations a slow body
Swings in space warm
Water pulled by the moon
Fog descends on the nostrils
Having died in its
Heart what pulse will
Ripen planes lift in dark
And move mice sleep
A sloth moves head down
The child sleeps
Guarded by an arrow
In what hour

Inversely, as the Square of their Distances Apart

It is impossible to see anything
In this dark; but I know this is me, Rexroth,
Plunging through the night on a chilling planet.
It is warm and busy in this vegetable
Darkness where invisible deer feed quietly.
The sky is warm and heavy, even the trees
Over my head cannot be distinguished,
But I know they are knobcone pines, that their cones
Endure unopened on the branches, at last
To grow imbedded in the wood, waiting for fire
To open them and reseed the burned forest.
And I am waiting, alone, in the mountains,
In the forest, in the darkness, and the world
Falls swiftly on its measured ellipse.

The Advantages of Learning

I am a man with no ambitions
And few friends, wholly incapable
Of making a living, growing no
Younger, fugitive from some just doom.
Lonely, ill-clothed, what does it matter?
At midnight I make myself a jug
Of hot white wine and cardamon seeds.
In a torn grey robe and old beret,
I sit in the cold writing poems,
Drawing nudes on the crooked margins,
Copulating with sixteen year old
Nymphomaniacs of my imagination.

Empire

Here I sit, reading the Stoic
Latin of Tacitus.
Tiberius sinks in senile
Gloom as Aeneas sank
In the smoky throat of Hades;
And the prose glitters like
A tray of dental instruments.
The toss head president,
Deep in his private catacomb,
Is preparing to pull
The trigger. His secretaries
Make speeches. In ten years
The art of communication
Will be more limited.
The wheel, the lever, the incline,
May survive, and perhaps,
The alphabet. At the moment
The intellectual
Advance guard is agitated
Over the relation
Between the Accumulation
Of Capital and the
Systematic Derangement of
The Senses, and the Right
To Homosexuality.

The Webs of Being

Climbing alone all day long
In the blazing waste of spring snow,
I came down with the sunset's edge
To the highest meadow, green
In the cold mist of waterfalls,
To a cobweb of water
Woven with innumerable
Bright flowers of wild iris;
And saw far down our fire's smoke
Rising between the canyon walls,
A human thing in the empty mountains.
And as I stood on the stones
In the midst of whirling water,
The whirling iris perfume
Caught me in a vision of you
More real than reality:
Fire in the deep curves of your hair;
Your hips whirled in a tango,
Out and back in dim scented light;
Your cheeks snow-flushed, the zithers
Ringing, all the crowded ski lodge
Dancing and singing; your arms
White in the brown autumn water,
Swimming through the fallen leaves,
Making a fluctuant cobweb
Of light on the sycamores;
Your thigh's exact curve, the fine gauze
Slipping through my hands, and you
Tense on the verge of abandon;
Your breasts' very touch and smell;
The sweet secret odor of sex.
Forever the thought of you,

And the splendor of the iris,
The crinkled iris petal,
The gold hairs powdered with pollen,
And the obscure cantata
Of the tangled water, and the
Burning, impassive snow peaks,
Are knotted together here.
This moment of fact and vision
Seizes immortality,
Becomes the person of this place.
The responsibility
Of love realized and beauty
Seen burns in a burning angel
Real beyond flower or stone.

The Signature of All Things

I

My head and shoulders, and my book
In the cool shade, and my body
Stretched bathing in the sun, I lie
Reading beside the waterfall –
Boehme's 'Signature of all Things'.
Through the deep July day the leaves
Of the laurel, all the colors
Of gold, spin down through the moving
Deep laurel shade all day. They float
On the mirrored sky and forest
For a while, and then, still slowly
Spinning, sink through the crystal deep
Of the pool to its leaf gold floor.
The saint saw the world as streaming
In the electrolysis of love.
I put him by and gaze through shade
Folded into shade of slender
Laurel trunks and leaves filled with sun.
The wren broods in her moss domed nest.
A newt struggles with a white moth
Drowning in the pool. The hawks scream,
Playing together on the ceiling
Of heaven. The long hours go by.
I think of those who have loved me,
Of all the mountains I have climbed,
Of all the seas I have swum in.
The evil of the world sinks.
My own sin and trouble fall away
Like Christian's bundle, and I watch
My forty summers fall like falling

Leaves and falling water held
Eternally in summer air.

2

Deer are stamping in the glades,
Under the full July moon.
There is a smell of dry grass
In the air, and more faintly,
The scent of a far off skunk.
As I stand at the wood's edge,
Watching the darkness, listening
To the stillness, a small owl
Comes to the branch above me,
On wings more still than my breath.
When I turn my light on him,
His eyes glow like drops of iron,
And he perks his head at me,
Like a curious kitten.
The meadow is bright as snow.
My dog prowls the grass, a dark
Blur in the blur of brightness.
I walk to the oak grove where
The Indian village was once.
There, in blotched and cobwebbed light
And dark, dim in the blue haze,
Are twenty Holstein heifers,
Black and white, all lying down,
Quietly together, under
The huge trees rooted in the graves.

3

When I dragged the rotten log
From the bottom of the pool,
It seemed heavy as stone.
I let it lie in the sun
For a month; and then chopped it
Into sections, and split them
For kindling, and spread them out
To dry some more. Late that night;
After reading for hours,
While moths rattled at the lamp,
The saints and the philosophers
On the destiny of man;
I went out on my cabin porch,
And looked up through the black forest
At the swaying islands of stars.
Suddenly I saw at my feet,
Spread on the floor of night, ingots
Of quivering phosphorescence,
And all about were scattered chips
Of pale cold light that was alive.

A Letter to
William Carlos Williams

Dear Bill,

When I search the past for you,
Sometimes I think you are like
St Francis, whose flesh went out
Like a happy cloud from him,
And merged with every lover –
Donkeys, flowers, lepers, suns –
But I think you are more like
Brother Juniper, who suffered
All indignities and glories
Laughing like a gentle fool.
You're in the Fioretti
Somewhere, for you're a fool, Bill,
Like the Fool in Yeats, the term
Of all wisdom and beauty.
It's you, stands over against
Helen in all her wisdom,
Solomon in all his glory.

Remember years ago, when
I told you you were the first
Great Franciscan poet since
The Middle Ages? I disturbed
The even tenor of dinner.
Your wife thought I was crazy.
It's true, though. And you're 'pure', too,
A real classic, though not loud
About it – a whole lot like
The girls of the Anthology.
Not like strident Sappho, who

For all her grandeur, must have
Had endemetriosis,
But like Anyte, who says
Just enough, softly, for all
The thousands of years to remember.

It's a wonderful quiet
You have, a way of keeping
Still about the world, and its
Dirty rivers, and garbage cans,
Red wheelbarrows glazed with rain,
Cold plums stolen from the icebox,
And Queen Anne's lace, and day's eyes,
And leaf buds bursting over
Muddy roads, and splotched bellies
With babies in them, and Cortes
And Malinche on the bloody
Causeway, the death of the flower world.

Nowadays, when the press reels
With chatterboxes, you keep still,
Each year a sheaf of stillness,
Poems that have nothing to say,
Like the stillness of George Fox,
Sitting still under the cloud
Of all the world's temptation,
By the fire, in the kitchen,
In the Vale of Beavor. And
The archtype, the silence
Of Christ, when he paused a long
Time and then said, 'Thou sayest it.'

Now in a recent poem you say,
'I who am about to die.'

Maybe this is just a tag
From the classics, but it sends
A shudder over me. Where
Do you get that stuff, Williams?
Look at here. The day will come
When a young woman will walk
By the lucid Williams River,
Where it flows through an idyllic
News from Nowhere sort of landscape,
And she will say to her children,
'Isn't it beautiful? It
Is named after a man who
Walked here once when it was called
The Passaic, and was filthy
With the poisonous excrements
Of sick men and factories.
He was a great man. He knew
It was beautiful then, although
Nobody else did, back there
In the Dark Ages. And the
Beautiful river he saw
Still flows in his veins, as it
Does in ours, and flows in our eyes,
And flows in time, and makes us
Part of it, and part of him.
That, children, is what is called
A sacramental relationship.
And that is what a poet
Is, children, one who creates
Sacramental relationships
That last always.'
With love and admiration,
Kenneth Rexroth.

For —

A MASSEUSE AND PROSTITUTE

Nobody knows what love is anymore.
Nobody knows what happened to God.
After midnight, the lesbians and fairies
Sweep through the streets of the old tenderloin,
Like spirochetes in a softening brain.
The hustlers have all been run out of town.
I look back on the times spent
Talking with you about the idiocies
Of a collapsing world and the brutalities
Of my race and yours,
While the sick, the perverted, the malformed,
Came and went, and you cooked them,
And rolled them, and beat them,
And sent them away with a little taste
Of electric life from the ends of your fingers.
Who could ever forget your amiable body,
Or your unruffled good sense,
Or your smiling sex?
I suppose your touch kept many men
As sane as they could be kept.
Every hour there is less of that touch in the world.

Took

take it bright day first hour
single chime clear water one thought
nobody has it
take age
take again
take anger
take anguish
point take point
or yellow collars question
take and take
nobody
nobody rode the sheep and has it
take nobody and got away nobody
so bright and salty
so bright and blue
young nobody has it
take girlish
and fans and blades
and glittering scales
take time
and mark it
dogged dogged
but what dogged
makes merry
takes and calves answers
each each
when the bears are polar
it all goes round and round
and rockets and rackets
take time take time
the time nobody ever had
take it all away take it far away

and
hide
it somewhere under the fine sand filled with shards of pots
    shaped like the torsos of splendor where everything is
    hidden and never will be deciphered and all the camels
    will die before anybody gets there and not one of the
    angels will ever come back
as
took

Gradualism

We slept naked
On top of the covers and woke
In the chilly dawn and crept
Between the warm sheets and made love
In the morning you said
'It snowed last night on the mountain'
High up on the dark basalt
Faint orange streaks of snow
In the ruddy dawn
I said
'It has been snowing for months
All over Canada and Alaska
And Minnesota and Michigan
Right now wet snow is falling
In the morning streets of Chicago
Bit by bit they are making over the world
Even in Mexico even for us'

Travellers in Erehwon

You open your
Dress on the dusty
Bed where no one
Has slept for years
An owl moans on the roof
You say
My dear my
Dear
In the smoky light of the old
Oil lamp your shoulders
Belly breasts buttocks
Are all like peach blossoms
Huge stars far away far apart
Outside the cracked window-pane
Immense immortal animals
Each one only an eye
Watch
You open your body
No end to the night
No end to the forest
House abandoned for a lifetime
In the forest in the night
No one will ever come
To the house
Alone
In the black world
In the country of eyes

Chinese Poems

1

Day after day the rain falls.
Week after week the grass grows.
Year after year the river flows.
Seventy years, seventy years,
The wheel of dreams revolves.

WANG HUNG KUNG

2

A thousand mountains without a bird.
Ten thousand miles with no trace of man.
A boat. An old man in a straw raincoat,
Alone in the snow, fishing in the freezing river.

LIU TSUNG-YUAN

3

I will always remember you
Entering the gate of childhood in the season
When plum blossoms give way to cherry blossoms.

WANG HUNG KUNG

Song from a Dance Play

I dream my love goes riding out
Upon a coal black mare.
A cloud of dark all about
Her – her floating hair.

She wears a short green velvet coat.
Her blouse is of red silk,
Open to her swan-like throat,
Her breasts white as milk.

Her skirt is of green velvet, too,
And shows her silken thigh,
Purple leather for her shoe,
Dark as her blue eye.

From her saddle grows a rose.
She rides in scented shade.
Silver birds sing as she goes
This song that she made:

'My father was a nightingale,
My mother a mermaid.
Honeyed notes that never fail
Upon my lips they laid.'

Poems from the Japanese

I wish I were close
To you as the wet skirt of
A salt girl to her body.
I think of you always.

AKAHITO

When I went out in
The Spring fields to pick
The young greens for you
Snow fell on my sleeves.

THE EMPEROR KŌKŌ

The white chrysanthemum
Is disguised by the first frost.
If I wanted to pick one
I could find it only by chance.

OSHIKOCHI NO MITSUNE

When she was still alive
We would go out, arm in arm,
And look at the elm trees
Growing on the embankment
In front of our house.
Their branches were interlaced.
Their crowns were dense with spring leaves.
They were like our love.

Love and trust were not enough to turn back
The wheels of life and death.
She faded like a mirage over the desert.

One morning like a bird she was gone
In the white scarves of death.
Now when the child
Whom she left in her memory
Cries and begs for her,
All I can do is pick him up
And hug him clumsily.
I have nothing to give him.
In our bedroom our pillows
Still lie side by side,
As we lay once.

I sit there by myself
And let the days grow dark.
I lie awake at night, sighing till daylight.
No matter how much I mourn
I shall never see her again.
They tell me her spirit
May haunt Mount Hagai
Under the eagles' wings.
I struggle over the ridges
And climb to the summit.
I know all the time

That I shall never see her,
Not even so much as a faint quiver in the air.
All my longing, all my love
Will never make any difference.

HITOMARO

When I went out
In the Spring meadows
To gather violets,
I enjoyed myself
So much that I stayed all night.

AKAHITO

The purity of the moonlight,
Falling out of the immense sky,
Is so great that it freezes
The water touched by its rays.

ANONYMOUS

The deer on pine mountain,
Where there are no falling leaves,
Knows the coming of autumn
Only by the sound of his own voice.

ONAKATOMI NO YOSHINOBU

In all the world
There is no way whatever.
The stag cries even
In the most remote mountain.

THE PRIEST
FUJIWARA NO TOSHINARI

WILLIAM CARLOS WILLIAMS

The Term

A rumpled sheet
of brown paper
about the length

and apparent bulk
of a man was
rolling with the

wind slowly over
and over in
the street as

a car drove down
upon it and
crushed it to

the ground. Unlike
a man it rose
again rolling

with the wind over
and over to be as
it was before.

To Waken an Old Lady

Old age is
a flight of small
cheeping birds
skimming
bare trees
above a snow glaze.
Gaining and failing
they are buffeted
by a dark wind –
But what?
On harsh weedstalks
the flock has rested,
The snow
is covered with broken
seedhusks
And the wind tempered
by a shrill
piping of plenty.

From 'Spring and All'

I

By thè road to the contagious hospital
under the surge of the blue
mottled clouds driven from the
northeast – a cold wind. Beyond, the
waste of broad, muddy fields
brown with dried weeds, standing and fallen

patches of standing water
the scattering of tall trees

All along the road the reddish
purplish, forked, upstanding, twiggy
stuff of bushes and small trees
with dead, brown leaves under them
leafless vines –

Lifeless in appearance, sluggish
dazed spring approaches –

They enter the new world naked,
cold, uncertain of all
save that they enter. All about them
the cold, familiar wind –

Now the grass, tomorrow
the stiff curl of wildcarrot leaf
One by one objects are defined –
It quickens: clarity, outline of leaf

But now the stark dignity of
entrance – Still, the profound change
has come upon them: rooted they
grip down and begin to awaken

To Elsie

The pure products of America
go crazy –
mountain folk from Kentucky

or the ribbed north end of
Jersey
with its isolate lakes and

valleys, its deaf-mutes, thieves
old names
and promiscuity between

devil-may-care men who have taken
to railroading
out of sheer lust of adventure –

and young slatterns, bathed
in filth
from Monday to Saturday

to be tricked out that night
with gauds
from imaginations which have no

peasant traditions to give them
character
but flutter and flaunt

sheer rags – succumbing without
emotion
save numbed terror

under some hedge of choke-cherry
or viburnum –
which they cannot express –

Unless it be that marriage
perhaps
with a dash of Indian blood

will throw up a girl so desolate
so hemmed round
with disease or murder

that she'll be rescued by an
agent –
reared by the state and

sent out at fifteen to work in
some hard-pressed
house in the suburbs –

some doctor's family, some Elsie –
voluptuous water
expressing with broken

brain the truth about us –
her great
ungainly hips and flopping breasts

addressed to cheap
jewelry
and rich young men with fine eyes

as if the earth under our feet
were
an excrement of some sky

and we degraded prisoners
destined
to hunger until we eat filth

while the imagination strains
after deer
going by fields of goldenrod in

the stifling heat of September
Somehow
it seems to destroy us

It is only in isolate flecks that
something
is given off

No one
to witness
and adjust, no one to drive the car

21

The Red Wheelbarrow

so much depends
upon

a red wheel
barrow

glazed with rain
water

beside the white
chickens

Proletarian Portrait

A big young bareheaded woman
in an apron

Her hair slicked back standing
on the street

One stockinged foot toeing
the sidewalk

Her shoe in her hand. Looking
intently into it

She pulls out the paper insole
to find the nail

That has been hurting her

The Locust Tree in Flower

Among
of
green

stiff
old
bright

broken
branch
come

white
sweet
May

again

Rain

As the rain falls
so does
     your love

bathe every
     open
object of the world –

In houses
the priceless dry
       rooms
of illicit love
where we live
hear the wash of the
       rain –

There
     paintings
and fine
     metalware
woven stuffs –
all the whorishness
of our
     delight
sees
from its window

the spring wash
of your love
     the falling
rain –

The trees
are become
beasts fresh risen
from
        the sea –
water

trickles
from the crevices of
their hides –

So my life is spent
                to keep out love
with which
she rains upon

                the world

of spring

            drips

so spreads

            the words

far apart to let in

                her love –

And running in between

the drops

> the rain

is a kind physician

> the rain
of her thoughts over
the ocean
> every

where

> walking with
invisible swift feet
over

> the helpless
> waves –

Unworldly love
that has no hope
> of the world

> and that
cannot change the world
to its delight –

> The rain
falls upon the earth
and grass and flowers

come
> perfectly

into form from its
                    liquid

clearness

            But love is
unworldly

            and nothing
comes of it but love

following
and falling endlessly
from
        her thoughts

Fine Work with Pitch and Copper

Now they are resting
in the fleckless light
separately in unison

like the sacks
of sifted stone stacked
regularly by twos

about the flat roof
ready after lunch
to be opened and strewn

The copper in eight
foot strips has been
beaten lengthwise

down the center at right
angles and lies ready
to edge the coping

One still chewing
picks up a copper strip
and runs his eye along it

Perpetuum Mobile: The City

                    – a dream
        we dreamed
                    each
        separately
                    we two

        of love
                    and of
        desire –

        that fused
        in the night –

        in the distance
                    over
        the meadows
                    by day
        impossible –
                    The city
        disappeared
                    when
        we arrived –

                    A dream
        a little false

        toward which
                    now
        we stand
                    and stare
        transfixed –

All at once
        in the east
rising!

        All white!

        small
as a flower –

a locust cluster
a shad bush
        blossoming

Over the swamps
        a wild
magnolia bud –
        greenish
white
a northern
        flower –
And so
        we live
        looking –

At night
        it wakes
On the black
        sky –

a dream
        toward which
we love –
at night
        more

than a little
        false –

We have bred
we have dug
we have figured up
our costs
we have bought
an old rug –

We batter at our
unsatisfactory
            brilliance –

There is no end
        to desire –

Let us break
            through
and go there –

in
        vain!

– delectable
        amusement:

Milling about –

Money! in
armored trucks –
Two men
        walking
at two paces from

      each other
their right hands
      at the hip –
on the butt of
an automatic –
till they themselves
hold up the bank
and themselves
      drive off
for themselves
      the money
in an armored car –

      For love!

Carefully
      carefully tying
carefully

      selected
wisps of long
dark hair
      wisp
by wisp
upon the stubs
of his kinky wool –
For two hours
      they worked –
      until
he coiled
      the thick
knot upon
that whorish
      head –

Dragged
      insensible
upon his face
by the lines –

– a running horse

For love.

Their eyes
      blown out –

– for love, for love!

Neither the rain
Nor the storm –
can keep them

      for love!

from the daily
accomplishment
    of their
appointed rounds –

Guzzling
the creamy foods
      while
out of sight
    in
the sub-cellar –
the waste fat
the old vegetables

chucked down
a chute
the foulest
sink in the world –

And go
on the out-tide
ten thousand
          cots
floating to sea
          like weed
that held back
the pristine ships –

And fattened there
an eel
in the water pipe –

          No end –

There!

          There!

There!

          – a dream
of lights
          hiding

the iron reason
          and stone
a settled
          cloud –

City

     whose stars
of matchless
     splendor –

     and
in bright-edged
     clouds
the moon –

     bring

silence

     breathlessly –

Tearful city
     on a summer's day
the hard grey
     dwindling
in a wall of
     rain –

     farewell!

Paterson (Early Draft): The Falls

What common language to unravel?
The Falls, combed into straight lines
from that rafter of a rock's
lip. Strike in! the middle of

some trenchant phrase, some
well packed clause. Then . . .
This is my plan. 4 sections: First,
the archaic persons of the drama.

An eternity of bird and bush,
resolved. An unraveling:
the confused streams aligned, side
by side, speaking! Sound

married to strength, a strength
of falling – from a height! The wild
voice of the shirt-sleeved
Evangelist rivaling, Hear

me! I am the Resurrection
and the Life! echoing
among the bass and pickerel, slim
eels from Barbados, Sargossa

Sea, working up the coast to that
bounty, ponds and wild streams –
Third, the old town: Alexander Hamilton
working up from St Croix,

from that sea! and a deeper, whence
he came! stopped cold

by that unmoving roar, fastened
there: the rocks silent

but the water, married to the stone,
voluble, though frozen; the water
even when and though frozen
still whispers and moans –

And in the brittle air
a factory bell clangs, at dawn, and
snow whines under their feet. Fourth,
the modern town, a

disembodied roar! the cataract and
its clamor broken apart – and from
all learning, the empty
ear struck from within, roaring   . .

Paterson: Episode 17 (Draft for Book III)

Beat hell out of it
    Beautiful Thing
      spotless cap
and crossed white straps
over the dark rippled cloth –
    Lift the stick
above that easy head
where you sit by the ivied
church, one arm
    buttressing you
long fingers spread out
among the clear grass prongs –
    and drive it down
    Beautiful Thing
that your caressing body kiss
    and kiss again
that holy lawn –

And again: obliquely –
legs curled under you as a
    deer's leaping –
pose of supreme indifference
    sacrament
to a summer's day
    Beautiful Thing
in the unearned suburbs
    then pause
    the arm fallen –
what memories
of what forgotten face
brooding upon that lily stem?

The incredible
nose straight from the brow
    the empurpled lips
and dazzled half-sleepy eyes
    Beautiful Thing
of some trusting animal
    makes a temple
of its place of savage slaughter
    revealing
the damaged will incites still
    to violence
consummately beautiful thing
and falls about your resting
    shoulders –

Gently! Gently!
as in all things an opposite
    that awakes
the fury, conceiving
    knowledge
by way of despair that has
    no place
to lay its glossy head –
Save only – Not alone!
    Never, if possible
alone! to escape the accepted
    chopping block
and a square hat! –

And as reverie gains and
    your joints loosen
    the trick's done!
Day is covered and we see you –
    but not alone!

drunk and bedraggled to release
the strictness of beauty
under a sky full of stars
    Beautiful Thing
and a slow moon –

        The car
    had stopped long since
    when the others
came and dragged those out
    who had you there
    indifferent
to whatever the anesthetic
    Beautiful Thing
might slum away the bars –
Reek of it!
    What does it matter?
    could set free
only the one thing –
But you!
– in your white lace dress
    'the dying swan'
and high heeled slippers – tall
as you already were –
    till your head
through fruitful exaggeration
was reaching the sky and the
prickles of its ecstasy
    Beautiful Thing!

And the guys from Paterson
    beat up
the guys from Newark and told
them to stay the hell out

of their territory and then
socked you one
    across the nose
    Beautiful Thing
for good luck and emphasis
    cracking it
till I must believe that all
desired women have had each
    in the end
    a busted nose
and live afterward marked up
    Beautiful Thing
    for memory's sake
to be credible in their deeds

Then back to the party!
    and they maled
and femaled you jealously
    Beautiful Thing
as if to discover when and
    by what miracle
there should escape what?
still to be possessed
out of what part
    Beautiful Thing
should it look?
    or be extinguished –
Three days in the same dress
    up and down –
    It would take
a Dominie to be patient
    Beautiful Thing
with you –

The stroke begins again –
    regularly
automatic
    contrapuntal to
the flogging
like the beat of famous lines
in the few excellent poems
    woven to make you
    gracious
and on frequent occasions
    foul drunk
    Beautiful Thing
pulse of release
    to the attentive
obedient mind.

To Ford Madox Ford in Heaven

Is it any better in Heaven, my friend Ford,
    than you found it in Provence?

I don't think so for you made Provence a
    heaven by your praise of it
to give a foretaste of what might be
    your joy in the present circumstances.
It was Heaven you were describing there
    transubstantiated from its narrowness
to resemble the paths and gardens of a
    greater world where you now reside.
But, dear man, you have taken a major
    part of it from us.
        Provence that you
praised so well will never be the same
    Provence to us
        now you are gone.

A heavenly man you seem to me now, never
    having been for me a saintly one.
It lived about you, a certain grossness that
    was not like the world.
The world is cleanly, polished and well
    made but heavenly man
is filthy with his flesh and corrupt that
    loves to eat and drink and whore –
to laugh at himself and not be afraid of
    himself knowing well he has
no possessions and opinions that are worth
    caring a broker's word about
and that all he is, but one thing, he feeds
    as one will feed a pet dog.

So roust and love and dredge the belly full
    in Heaven's name!
I laugh to think of you wheezing in Heaven.
    Where is Heaven? But why
do I ask that, since you showed the way?
    I don't care a damn for it
other than for that better part lives beside
    me here so long as I
live and remember you. Thank God you
    were not delicate, you let the world in
and lied! damn it you lied grossly
    sometimes. But it was all, I
see now, a carelessness, the part of a man
    that is homeless here on earth.

Provence, the fat assed Ford will never
    again strain the chairs of your cafés,
pull and pare for his dish your sacred garlic,
    grunt and sweat and lick
his lips. Gross as the world he has left to
    us he has become
a part of that of which you were the known
    part, Provence, he loved so well.

Song

beauty is a shell
from the sea
where she rules triumphant
till love has had its way with her

scallops and
lion's paws
sculptured to the
tune of retreating waves

undying accents
repeated till
the ear and the eye lie
down together in the same bed

Heel & Toe to the End

Gagarin says, in ecstasy,
he could have
gone on forever

he floated
ate and sang
and when he emerged from that

one hundred eight minutes off
the surface of
the earth he was smiling

Then he returned
to take his place
among the rest of us

from all that division and
subtraction a measure
toe and heel

heel and toe he felt
as if he had
been dancing

From 'Asphodel, That Greeny Flower'

BOOK I

Of asphodel, that greeny flower,
       like a buttercup
              upon its branching stem –
save that it's green and wooden –
       I come, my sweet,
            to sing to you.
We lived long together
       a life filled,
            if you will,
with flowers. So that
       I was cheered
            when I came first to know
that there were flowers also
       in hell.
            Today
I'm filled with the fading memory of those flowers
       that we both loved,
            even to this poor
colorless thing –
       I saw it
            when I was a child –
little prized among the living
       but the dead see,
            asking among themselves:
What do I remember
       that was shaped
            as this thing is shaped?
while our eyes fill
       with tears.
            Of love, abiding love

it will be telling
      though too weak a wash of crimson
         colors it
to make it wholly credible.
      There is something
         something urgent
I have to say to you
      and you alone
         but it must wait
while I drink in
      the joy of your approach,
         perhaps for the last time.
And so
      with fear in my heart
         I drag it out
and keep on talking
      for I dare not stop.
         Listen while I talk on
against time.
      It will not be
         for long.
I have forgot   .
      and yet I see clearly enough
         something
central to the sky
      which ranges round it.
         An odor
springs from it!
      A sweetest odor!
         Honeysuckle! And now
there comes the buzzing of a bee!
      and a whole flood
         of sister memories!
Only give me time,

time to recall them
before I shall speak out.
Give me time,
time.
When I was a boy
I kept a book
to which, from time
to time,
I added pressed flowers
until, after a time,
I had a good collection.
The asphodel,
forebodingly,
among them.
I bring you,
reawakened,
a memory of those flowers.
They were sweet
when I pressed them
and retained
something of their sweetness
a long time.
It is a curious odor,
a moral odor,
that brings me
near to you.
The color
was the first to go.
There had come to me
a challenge,
your dear self,
mortal as I was,
the lily's throat
to the hummingbird!

Endless wealth,
      I thought,
            held out its arms to me.
A thousand topics
      in an apple blossom.
            The generous earth itself
gave us lief.
      The whole world
            became my garden!
But the sea
      which no one tends
            is also a garden
when the sun strikes it
      and the waves
            are wakened.
I have seen it
      and so have you
            when it puts all flowers
to shame.
      Too, there are the starfish
            stiffened by the sun
and other sea wrack
      and weeds. We knew that
            along with the rest of it
for we were born by the sea,
      knew its rose hedges
            to the very water's brink.
There the pink mallow grows
      and in their season
            strawberries
and there, later,
      we went to gather
            the wild plum.
I cannot say

that I have gone to hell
                    for your love
but often
            found myself there
                        in your pursuit.
I do not like it
            and wanted to be
                        in heaven. Hear me out.
Do not turn away.

I have learned much in my life
            from books
                        and out of them
about love.
            Death
                        is not the end of it.
There is a hierarchy
            which can be attained,
                        I think,
in its service.
            Its guerdon
                        is a fairy flower;
a cat of twenty lives.
            If no one came to try it
                        the world
would be the loser.
            It has been
                        for you and me
as one who watches a storm
            come in over the water.
                        We have stood
from year to year
            before the spectacle of our lives
                        with joined hands.

The storm unfolds.
      Lightning
          plays about the edges of the clouds.
The sky to the north
      is placid,
           blue in the afterglow
as the storm piles up.
      It is a flower
          that will soon reach
the apex of its bloom.

The Descent

The descent beckons
        as the ascent beckoned.
                Memory is a kind
of accomplishment,
        a sort of renewal
           even
an initiation, since the spaces it opens are new places
        inhabited by hordes
              heretofore unrealized,
of new kinds –
        since their movements
            are toward new objectives
(even though formerly they were abandoned).

No defeat is made up entirely of defeat – since
the world it opens is always a place
        formerly
            unsuspected. A
world lost,
        a world unsuspected,
           beckons to new places
and no whiteness (lost) is so white as the memory
of whiteness   .

With evening, love wakens
        though its shadows
           which are alive by reason
of the sun shining –
        grow sleepy now and drop away
           from desire   .

Love without shadows stirs now
            beginning to awaken
                        as night
advances.

The descent
            made up of despairs
                      and without accomplishment
realizes a new awakening:
                 which is a reversal
of despair.
            For what we cannot accomplish, what
is denied to love,
            what we have lost in the anticipation –
                 a descent follows,
endless and indestructible   .

MORE ABOUT PENGUINS

Penguin Book News, which appears every month, contains details of all the new books issued by Penguins as they are published. From time to time it is supplemented by *Penguins in Print*, which is a complete list of all books published by Penguins which are in print. (There are nearly three thousand of these.)

A specimen copy of *Penguin Book News* will be sent to you free on request, and you can become a subscriber for the price of the postage – 3s. for a year's issues (including the complete lists). Just write to Dept EP, Penguin Books Ltd, Harmondsworth, Middlesex, enclosing a cheque or postal order, and your name will be added to the mailing list.

Some other books published by Penguins are described on the following pages.

Note: *Penguin Book News* and *Penguins in Print* are not available in the U.S.A. or Canada

The New Poetry

Selected and introduced by

A. ALVAREZ

'This is a personal anthology. It makes no claims to give a sample of every kind of verse now being written in Great Britain. I am, however, trying to represent what I think is the most significant work of the British poets who began to come into their own in the fifties. I have also included the work of four American writers who, although established before then, seem, as I try to explain in the Introduction, to be concerned with problems that some of the new generation of poets over here are beginning to face.

This is not, in short, an anthology for the reader who wants a complete guide to the contemporary poetic scene; but then, anyone who wants that already has a large number of excellent collections from which to choose. In this book I am, instead, simply attempting to give my idea of what, that really matters, has happened to poetry in England during the last decade' – A. Alvarez

The Penguin Book of Animal Verse

GEORGE MACBETH

'I am on the side of those who tend to like poems about dogs because they like dogs rather than because they like poems,' writes George MacBeth in his introduction. This anthology is also for those who like cats, horses, mice, squirrels, otters, elephants – and poetry. It includes every kind of animal and every kind of poet.

Some of the poems are narrative – Waller's exciting *Battle of the Summer Islands* about two whales fighting for their lives, or D. J. Enright's *The Quagga*; some poems are descriptive – D. H. Lawrence's *Kangaroo* with 'Her little loose hands, and drooping Victorian shoulders'; some are funny – Leigh Hunt's *To a Fish*: 'You strange, astonished-looking, angle-faced, Dreary-mouthed, gaping wretches of the sea'. But in all of them one is aware that poets write about animals with a special sympathy, showing us that we enjoy animals most for their likeness to ourselves. Carl Sandburg writes, 'There is a wolf in me . . . There is a fox in me . . . There is an eagle in me and a mocking-bird . . . Oh, I got a zoo, I got a menagerie, inside my ribs . . .'

Arranged alphabetically, *Animal Verse* is an encyclopedic collection of animal poems written between medieval times and today. 104 poets are represented.

NOT FOR SALE IN THE U.S.A.

The Mid Century
English Poetry 1940–60

INTRODUCED AND EDITED BY DAVID WRIGHT

Poets represented in this collection:

Auden	Philip Larkin
Betjeman	Christopher Logue
Empson	Dom Moraes
Graves	Charles Tomlinson
MacNeice	Anthony Thwaite
Stevie Smith	George Barker
Vernon Watkins	Thomas Blackburn
Donald Davie	Charles Causley
Thom Gunn	David Gascoyne
Michael Hamburger	W. S. Graham
Brian Higgins	John Heath-Stubbs
Geoffrey Hill	Patrick Kavanagh
Ted Hughes	Dylan Thomas
Elizabeth Jennings	etc.

NOT FOR SALE IN THE U.S.A.

Penguin Modern European Poets

CAVAFY; ELYTIS; GATSOS; SEFERIS
Selected Poems

Penguin Modern European Poets is designed to present, in verse translations, the work of significant European poets of this century for readers unfamiliar with the original languages. The series already includes Yevtushenko, Rilke, Apollinaire, Prévert, and Quasimodo.

This volume contains translations of a selection of modern Greek poetry. Of the four authors, two are established poets with international reputations, one is already well-known in Greece, and one, the youngest, shows promise of achieving an international standing in time.

NOT FOR SALE IN THE U.S.A.

YEVTUSHENKO
Selected Poems

Yevgeny Yevtushenko is the fearless spokesman of his generation in Russia. In verse that is young, fresh and outspoken he frets at restraint and injustice, as in his now famous protest over the Jewish pogrom at Kiev.

But he can write lyrically, too, of the simple things of humanity – love, a birthday, a holiday in Georgia. And in 'Zima Junction' he brilliantly records his impressions on a visit to his home in Siberia.

Longer Contemporary Poems

Edited with an Introduction by David Wright

This collection includes poems by

W. H. AUDEN
W. S. GRAHAM
PATRICK KAVANAGH
ANDREW YOUNG
GEORGE BARKER
HUGH MACDIARMID
PETER LEVI
ANTHONY CRONIN
VERNON WATKINS

The Penguin Modern Poets

PENGUIN MODERN POETS 9

D97